What Educators Should Know About Copyright

by
Virginia M. Helm

Library of Congress Catalog Card Number 85-63688
ISBN 0-87367-233-X
Copyright © 1986 by the Phi Delta Kappa Educational Foundation
Bloomington, Indiana

This fastback is sponsored by the Clearwater-St. Petersburg Chapter of Phi Delta Kappa, which made a generous contribution toward publication costs.

Table of Contents

Introduction 7

The Copyright Law and Fair Use 9
  Rights of Copyright Proprietors 10
  Limitations on Exclusive Rights 11
  Fair Use: Statutory Factors 11
  Fair Use: Other Factors 13
  The Supreme Court and Fair Use 14

Guidelines for Photocopying 18
  Single Copying for Teachers and Researchers 18
  Multiple Copies for Classroom Use 19
  Prohibited Copying 20
  Another Option: Permission from Publishers 20
  Copying Music 21
  Photocopying by Library Staff 21

Computers and Copyright 24
  Copyright and Software Use 27
  Other Questioned Uses 31
  School Libraries and Computer Software 31

Copyright Law and Audiovisual Materials 33
  Permissible Uses 33
  Prohibited Uses 34
  Videotapes: The "For Home Use Only" Warning 35
  School Libraries and Videotapes 36
  School Libraries and Other Audiovisual Materials 37

Videotape Recorders: Off-Air Taping 39
  Guidelines for Taping Commercial Broadcasts 39
  Guidelines for Taping Public Broadcasting Service Programs 41
  Television Broadcasts Taped by Teachers 42

Live and Transmitted Performances 44
   Live Performances... 44
   Transmitted Performances 45

Penalties for Infringement of Copyright 46

Conclusion 48

References 50

Introduction

Schools have had such "low-tech" machines as typewriters and film-strip projectors for many years; but they posed few, if any, legal problems for educators. Now educators are blessed – or confronted – with "high tech" photocopy machines, microcomputers, videocassette recorders, and closed-circuit, satellite, and cable TV. With the advancement from mechanical to electronic technology, teaching has become complicated not only technologically but also legally.

The accessibility of advanced technology poses new and frustrating challenges for educators. Because so many educational materials can be duplicated easily, it is imperative that educators be familiar with the copyright regulations on use of technological hardware and software. If ethical considerations are not sufficient motivation for educators to use technology legally, practical considerations should be; for the industries that produce copyrighted materials used in schools are becoming increasingly aggressive about protecting their interests against violations.

How many educators violate copyright law every day as they use these technological wonders? If faced with charges of copyright infringement, how many would plead ignorance? How many would cite the altruistic motive of providing otherwise inaccessible materials to their students while saving tax dollars? And how many would expect either motive to be an adequate defense in the courtroom?

Whether duplicating computer software, films, or videotapes without authorization or illegally showing television broadcasts taped off the air, educators engaged in such copyright violations endanger themselves and their enterprise in two ways. First, they unquestionably render themselves liable to prosecution for copyright infringement. Second, they may jeopardize the creation of future educational materials by depriving producers of these materials of profits, without which they cannot continue to create new materials.

To minimize these potential dangers, educators must first become familiar with the basics of copyright law discussed in this fastback. This includes a general understanding of the doctrine of "fair use" and its applicability for research, scholarship, and classroom uses. Next, educators must become knowledgeable about the various sets of guidelines established to determine fair use in photocopying and videotaping commercial and public broadcasting television programs. Third, educators need to understand how the courts have interpreted the copyright law and derivative guidelines. Finally, educators must be aware of the existence of licensing agreements and, more importantly, become familiar with any licenses regulating the use of technological equipment, audiovisual materials, or computer software in their own district. Reading this fastback will provide educators with basic information on copyright regulations. The references at the end of the fastback provide more complete information.

The Copyright Law and Fair Use

It may surprise many educators to learn that the primary intent of the federal copyright law is not to protect the economic interests of authors and artists; its primary purpose, articulated by the Copyright Office after the Copyrights Act was revised in 1976, is to promote the creation and dissemination of knowledge and ideas. The Constitution (Article I, Section 8, Clause 8) specifies the purpose of copyright protection: "To promote the progress of science and useful arts." Today, this phrase is interpreted more broadly as advancing the general welfare by encouraging the pursuit and dissemination of intellectual and artistic works.

Those creative individuals who produce intellectual and artistic works deserve reasonable reward for their efforts. Therefore, copyright legislation is intended to provide incentive and to protect the financial interests of creative individuals by prohibiting others from copying or otherwise misusing their works.

In theory, the interests of copyright owners and those of the public should complement each other; in fact, they are often in conflict. Congress has tried to balance these sometimes conflicting interests, although its efforts to date are more a compromise than a resolution to the problem. As with most compromises, nobody is entirely happy with the outcome; though few are as cynical as Mark Twain, who observed, "Only one thing is impossible for God: to find any sense in any copyright law on the planet."

Conflicts over copyright occur among many groups, but nowhere are the restrictions on access to copyrighted material felt more keenly than in schools and colleges. Teachers and administrators want to provide students with access to costly copyrighted books, articles, audiovisual materials, and computer software. Why, they ask, can we not reproduce educational materials when neither we nor the students will profit financially and when we would not otherwise purchase those materials because of lack of funds? Isn't it detrimental to the advancement of knowledge to limit the students' access to educational materials merely because of copyright restrictions?

Not all reproduction of copyrighted material is illegal, but there are numerous qualifications for every privilege or exemption granted. Just what rights are provided for copyright owners? What rights, in turn, are provided for educators wanting or needing to use copyrighted works? The answers to these and related questions are discussed below.

Rights of Copyright Proprietors

Individuals who want to protect their written, audio, or visual work must follow certain procedures to copyright their work. It is possible to copyright one's work as soon as it is "fixed in a tangible medium" simply by placing a copyright notice on all copies of the work. That notice must include the name of the copyright owner, the year of publication, and the symbol © or the word "copr." or "copyright." However, the copyright must be *registered* and two copies of the work deposited with the Copyright Office before the author can seek remedies for copyright infringement.

Once copyright is obtained, that individual becomes a copyright owner or proprietor. At that point, the copyright proprietor acquires the exclusive rights to engage in and to authorize the following activities:

1. reproduce copies of the work;
2. prepare derivative works based on the copyrighted work;
3. distribute copies of the work by sale, rental, lease, or lending;
4. publicly perform the work (if it is a literary, musical, dramatic, or choreographic work or a pantomime, motion picture, or audiovisual work);

5. publicly display the work (if it is a literary, musical, dramatic, choreographic, sculptural, graphic, or pictorial work — including the individual images of a film — or a pantomime).

These exclusive rights provide considerable protection against the possibility of other individuals obtaining a copy of a copyrighted work and using it for their own profit without the consent of the copyright proprietor. However, while these rights are exclusive, they are not absolute or without restrictions.

Limitations on Exclusive Rights

If copyright owners possessed the above exclusive rights without any limitations, their own welfare might suffer. Readers and theater patrons would be deprived of the excerpts from books and televised film clips used by reviewers. More significant to the public welfare is the need to make copyrighted material available to scholars, researchers, and teachers, which will ultimately benefit society.

In response to this concern for the public welfare, Congress has incorporated into the Copyrights Act a number of limitations on the exclusive rights of copyright owners. Some of the limitations are specific to the kind of work (audiovisual works, computer programs, sound recordings) or to the repository of the copyrighted materials (libraries, media centers, various data bases). A more general limitation is known as "fair use," which is applicable to copyrighted works in all media. The concept of fair use, which is of primary importance to educators, is discussed below followed by an examination of the work-specific limitations for various technologies.

Fair Use: Statutory Factors

The fair use provision is found in Section 107 of the 1976 Copyrights Act and is the first statutory version of a judicial doctrine dating back more than 100 years. It is intended to balance the interests of copyright owners with the needs of others for access to copyrighted material. Educators are the prime but not the sole beneficiaries of this provision; limited access is also available to scholars, researchers, news reporters, and media critics.

In determing fair use, the following four factors are considered:

1. The *purpose and character* of the use, including whether the copied material will be for nonprofit, educational, or commercial use. This factor at first seems reassuring; but unfortunately for educators, several courts have held that absence of financial gain is insufficient for a finding of fair use.

2. The *nature* of the copyrighted work, with special consideration given to the distinction between a creative work and an informational work. For example, photocopies made of a newspaper or newsmagazine column are more likely to be considered a fair use than copies made of a musical score or a short story. Duplication of material originally developed for classroom consumption is *less* likely to be a fair use than is the duplication of materials prepared for public consumption. For example, a teacher who photocopies a workbook page or a textbook chapter is depriving the copyright owner of profits more directly than if copying one page from the daily paper.

3. The *amount, substantiality, or portion* used in relation to the copyrighted work as a whole. This factor requires consideration of 1) the proportion of the larger work that is copied and used, and 2) the significance of the copied portion. Reproduction of 10 lines copied from a 20-line poem is qualitatively different from the reproduction of 10 lines from a 20-page story or a 200-page book. And 10 lines containing the "essence" of a literary work is regarded differently than 10 lines selected and reproduced to illustrate a less significant point. Many courts have found that reproduction of an entire work automatically renders the use unfair, though that interpretation has recently been rejected by several federal courts.

4. The effect of the use on the *potential market* of the copyrighted work. This factor is regarded by many copyright experts as the most critical one in determining fair use; and it serves as the basic principle from which the other three factors are derived and to which they are related. If the reproduction of a copyrighted work reduces the potential market and sales and, therefore, the potential profits of the copyright owner, that use is unlikely to be found a fair use.

These four factors in Section 107 are not the only factors used in determining fair use, and there is no consensus among copyright experts concerning their relevance for the technology of the 1980s. Section 107 derives directly from an 1841 case, when only printed material was an issue; and it has been characterized by at least one noted scholar as "stilted and anachronistic." But whether outdated by new technology or not, the four factors in the fair use provision of Section 107 have come to be applied in a much more rigid way than Congress intended. Legislative history indicates that these four factors were meant to be illustrative, but they seem to have become determinative. Since the enactment of Section 107, courts have tended to limit their assessment of fair use to only these four factors. This is unfortunate because a number of other significant criteria were developed and applied by the courts before 1976.

Fair Use: Other Factors

Before the 1976 Copyrights Act, fair use was a flexible common-law doctrine; and courts developed and applied relevant criteria to each case, thereby adding to the list of possible factors in determining fair use. Since there is nothing prohibiting future reliance on these factors, a few of the most significant ones are presented briefly.

1. *Functional Use Test.* This test, sometimes called the "substitute effect test," can be used as a way of applying the fourth fair use factor: the effect on market value or economic harm. To the extent that a copied work is used to substitute for a purchased copy, it is more likely to diminish the copyright owner's profits. And, of course, it is most likely to substitute for a purchased copy when it has been reproduced in its entirety. While the relevance of this consideration is somewhat mitigated by recent Supreme Court rulings, any time educators use copied material in a very different way than a purchased copy would be used, they increase the likelihood of a fair use finding.

2. *Productive Use Test.* The term *productive* is used in two different ways. The first and less common meaning is a use of copyrighted material that creates a new work. In this context, incorporating excerpts into an original literary or artistic work would be a productive use. The second, more frequent meaning of *productive* refers to a use that produces some ultimate benefit to society. A productive use should

be contrasted with a convenient use; mere convenience has never been considered an adequate rationale for fair use (with one exception, the *Sony* decision, discussed below).

3. *Public Interest Factor.* Closely related to the productive use test is the public interest factor, which, under the rubric of the "nature of the work" fair use factor, is increasingly considered by courts attempting to balance the interests of copyright owners with the interests of the public good. This factor most often has involved the use by one author of another author's copyrighted materials rather than use by teachers in the classroom, but its relevance for researchers and educators is obvious. Application of the public interest factor requires asking the question, "Is a legitimate public interest served by the use or distribution of this copyrighted work?" While defining public interest always will involve a subjective judgment, recent court decisions generally have identified public interest as having "the fullest information available." When applying this factor, the greater the degree of public interest, the greater protection is likely to be afforded the use or distribution of copyrighted material. However, legal scholars warn that heavy reliance on this factor will seriously erode copyright protection, and they urge that greater consideration be given to whether duplicated copyrighted materials *need* to be used.

4. *The Availability Test.* The availability of copyrighted material was initially suggested as a factor affecting fair use during the 1964 copyright amendment hearings. It also was a decisive factor in the 1982 *Encyclopaedia Britannica Educational Corp.* v. *Crooks* (BOCES) case, in which the court held that the extensive and systematic off-air taping of television broadcasts by a state educational service agency for distribution to school districts was illegal, at least in part, because the broadcasting companies made their programs available for short-term rental. On the other hand, if the work is not readily available for purchase or through normal channels, the court suggested that copying the work is more likely to constitute a fair use.

The Supreme Court and Fair Use

In 1984 in *Sony Corp. of America* v. *Universal City Studios, Inc.*, commonly known as the Betamax case, the Supreme Court upheld the right of individuals to make off-air videotapings of television programs. Perhaps more significant than the ruling itself is the reasoning on which the ruling was based. Two positions developed by the Court are likely to serve as precedents in future cases involving fair use.

First, in *Sony* the Supreme Court proclaimed fair use to be a noninfringing use, not merely a defense against infringement. The result of this distinction is to shift the burden of proof from the user/defendant to the copyright owner/plaintiff, who must now demonstrate either actual or potential harm. Furthermore, the Supreme Court weighted heavily the importance of dissemination and public access in the balancing test that derives from the fair use provision. This provides much-needed direction to future applications of fair use and should be encouraging to educators, who will benefit from this more liberal interpretation and application of fair use.

The *Sony* case has significant implications for the future application of the four fair use factors. Specifically, in applying the first factor, the Court held that the noncommercial, nonprofit character of off-air taping in the home led to a presumption of fair use. That presumption of fair use necessarily and explicitly reduced the significance of factors two and three in Section 107, as did the timeshifting involved in videotaping a television program for later viewing. Timeshifting, in fact, "merely enables a viewer to see such a work which he had been invited to witness in its entirety free of charge," so that "the fact that the entire work is reproduced . . . does not have its ordinary effect of militating against a finding of fair use." In short, the second factor (the nature of the work) and the third factor (the extent of copying) were held to be negligible if not immaterial considerations.

The fourth factor, the effect on the potential market, also received special emphasis in *Sony*. In its discussion of this factor, the Court reiterated a legal principle incorporated in a number of earlier lower court decisions, that is, commercial use is an infringement but "noncommercial uses are a different matter." A copyright holder must now show either that "the particular use is harmful" or by a preponderance of the evidence that "*some* meaningful likelihood of future harm exists." This shift in the burden of proof may prove helpful to defendant educators, who in the past often bore the burden of proving that they *did not* negatively affect the potential market or value of the copyrighted work.

In a 1975 case, *Williams & Wilkins Co.* v. *U.S.*, the Supreme Court affirmed (in a 4/4 decision) a lower court ruling that reproduction of entire articles may sometimes be protected by the fair use doctrine. The defendants in this case reproduced thousands of articles for the National Institute of Health and for the National Library of Medicine; these articles were provided at cost to physicians and medical researchers. The courts weighed the economic harm to the publishers of the journals from which articles were photocopied against the public welfare advanced by medical research and found that "medical science will be hurt if such photocopying is stopped." It should be noted that the publishers' case was harmed as much by failure to provide evidence of any actual or potential economic harm as by the conclusion that medical science warranted greater protection than did their economic interests.

The *Williams & Wilkins* decision was made before the 1976 Copyrights Act and its photocopying guidelines were incorporated into the legislative history of that act. Despite an equally divided Supreme Court, which renders the decision binding only in the jurisdiction of the lower court, *Williams & Wilkins* is important because two central considerations in that case were the same central considerations in *Sony*. Specifically, in *Williams & Wilkins* the courts emphasized the nonprofit, private use by researchers of the reproduced material and the lack of demonstrated economic harm suffered by the plaintiff. They also decided that fair use may sometimes permit reproduction of a copyrighted work in its entirety.

The Supreme Court finally has provided some much-needed direction for courts facing fair use issues in the future. Educators can find some encouragement in the Court's heavy and almost exclusive weighting of the first and fourth factors of fair use. Nonprofit uses carry a presumption of fair use and therefore the plaintiff must prove actual or likely potential economic harm. However, that does not mean that any and all educational uses are automatically legalized, for there are other statutory provisions and congressionally approved sets of guidelines regulating a variety of materials. *The fair use section of the copyright law is applicable in situations not otherwise governed by these additional statutory provisions and guidelines*, which are discussed in the following chapters.

Guidelines for Photocopying

Vaguely aware of the existence of restrictions on photocopying, many educators feel uneasy when they photocopy *anything* for use in the classroom. However, educators in nonprofit education institutions may photocopy part or all of almost any copyrighted work as long as they follow the federally adopted guidelines. These guidelines permit more extensive copying for use by a single educator in his or her research or preparation for teaching.

The information that follows is drawn from "Guidelines For Classroom Copying in Nonprofit Educational Institutions." These guidelines were written by a group representing educators, authors, and publishers and were incorporated into the report of the House Judiciary Committee; as such, they are part of the legislative history of the Copyright Act, although they do not have the force of law. They also are prefaced by the statement: "There may be instances in which copying which does not fall within the guidelines stated below may nonetheless be permitted under the criteria of fair use." In short, these guidelines are neither rigidly definitive nor are they accorded the status of law. Legally they are considered advisory, but they do offer reassurance that users who follow them will be able to argue a "good faith" fair use.

Single Copying for Teachers and Researchers

Researchers or teachers preparing to teach a class may make or request to have made a single copy of: 1) a book chapter; 2) an article from a newspaper or periodical; 3) a short story, essay, or short poem; or 4) a chart, graph, diagram, cartoon, drawing, or picture from a book, periodical, or newspaper.

Multiple Copies for Classroom Use

Teachers may duplicate enough copies to provide one copy for each student in a course, as long as each copy includes a notice of copyright and as long as they meet three tests: the brevity test, the spontaneity test, and the cumulative effect test.

1. *Brevity Test.* For poetry, the suggested maximum is 250 words. Poems containing fewer than 250 words may be copied in their entirety (provided that they are not printed on more than two pages), and excerpts up to 250 words are permissible from longer poems.

For prose, the guidelines offer two different limitations. Educators may copy any *complete* story, essay, or article under 2,500 words or *excerpts* of not more than 1,000 words or 10% of the work, whichever is less. However, certain shorter works designated as "special" because they contain illustrations (for example, children's stories) may not be copied in their entirety even though they have less than 2,500 words. From these special works educators may not copy more than two of the published pages containing no more than 10% of the text.

For illustrations, the guidelines suggest no more than one chart, graph, diagram, drawing, cartoon, or picture per book or periodical issue.

2. *Spontaneity Test.* The "inspiration and decision to use the work" must occur so soon prior to classroom use that it would not be feasible to write for and receive permission from the publisher to duplicate the material. It also is imperative that the copying occur at the request of the teacher, not at the directive of an administrator or other "higher authority."

3. *Cumulative Effect Test.* Generally, only one copy may be made of a short poem, article, story, or essay. No more than three of these items may be from the same collective work or periodical volume during one class term. The most limiting restriction further specifies no more than a total of nine instances of such multiple copying for one

course during one class term. Finally, all multiple copying of a particular work is limited to one course; in other words, copying a work to be used in several courses is not likely to be considered a fair use of the material.

Prohibited Copying

Although the guidelines permit limited copying for varying purposes, some uses are prohibited regardless of the otherwise permissible copying. Specifically, educators are not to create through photocopying their own anthologies, compilations, or collective works whether brought together in one collection or reproduced and used separately. Furthermore, any copying must not substitute for the purchase of books, periodicals, or reprints; this prohibition especially applies to the duplication of "consumable" materials such as workbooks, test booklets, and standardized tests. Students must not be charged more than the actual cost of copying the material. Finally, and of special importance, a teacher must not duplicate the same item from one term to another.

Another Option: Permission from Publishers

While limitations contained in the guidelines may seem overly restrictive to some educators, they should keep in mind that these limitations only apply to copying *without permission* from the publisher. When need dictates duplication and use of copyrighted material beyond the scope of copying permitted by the guidelines, educators always have the option of writing to the publisher for permission to make multiple copies. Such requests for permission should include:

1. title, author(s) or editor(s), edition number;
2. exact amount (pages) of material used, preferably including a photocopy of the material involved in the request;
3. number of copies to be made;
4. description of how the material will be used, for what course or other purpose, and frequency of use if for more than one occasion;
5. process of duplication (photocopy, offset, ditto).

Copying Music

The guidelines for educational uses of photocopied music, like those for copying prose and poetry, were incorporated into the report of the House Judiciary Committee and provide authoritative if not legally binding standards for fair use. Many of the same principles apply to the duplication of both the written word and music. Specifically, educators are permitted to make copies of music in an emergency, understood as the need to "replace purchased copies which for any reason are not available for an imminent performance" as long as replacement copies are purchased later.

For academic purposes other than performance, a teacher preparing for a class or a researcher may duplicate a *single copy* of an "entire performable unit (section, movement, aria, etc.)" if that unit is unavailable except in a larger work and if it is out of print, as confirmed by the copyright proprietor. For other nonperformance educational purposes, *multiple copies* of no more than 10% of the whole work may be made as long as the excerpt does not comprise a performable unit. Such multiple copying should not exceed one copy per student.

Furthermore, printed copies of purchased music may be edited or simplified; but this privilege does not extend to the alteration or addition of lyrics. Teachers may make a single copy of a sound recording of copyrighted music for use in "constructing aural exercises or examinations," though the guidelines specify that this applies "to the copyright of the music itself and not to any copyright which may exist in the sound recording."

Educators are not allowed to copy music "to create or replace or substitute for anthologies, compilations or collective works." Also, as with prose and poetry, copied music is not to be substituted for the purchase of music except for emergency situations and for excerpts as described above.

Photocopying by Library Staff

Section 108 of the Copyrights Act permits library employees to make a *single* copy of a work as long as the library 1) receives no direct or indirect financial gain; 2) is either open to the public or, if a restricted archives or library, is available to researchers not affiliated with that institution; and 3) affixes notice of copyright on all duplicated works.

Having met the above requirements, a library may still make copies only under certain circumstances. First, it may duplicate in facsimile form a published, copyrighted work that is damaged, deteriorating, lost, or stolen if a reasonable effort uncovers no possibility for replacement at a fair price. Second, library staff may duplicate *small excerpts* from copyrighted works or "no more than one article or other contribution to a copyrighted collection or periodical issue" for another library or archives or for an individual requesting the copy for research or scholarship purposes. In order to legally duplicate *substantial excerpts* or *entire works* at the request of users or other libraries, the library must first conduct a reasonable investigation to determine whether a copy of the copyrighted work can be otherwise obtained at a fair price. In any of these circumstances, the library must post in a place prominent to users a warning of copyright. As long as the required warning of copyright is prominently displayed, library employees are granted immunity against charges of infringement for copyright violations committed by users of unsupervised photocopy machines or other reproducing equipment.

Although libraries are permitted "isolated and unrelated" reproduction of a single copy of the same work on separate occasions, Section 108(g) does prohibit 1) "related or concerted reproduction" of multiple copies of the same material and 2) "systematic reproduction . . . of single or multiple copies" of articles. However, even these prohibitions are qualified in that libraries may participate in interlibrary arrangements as long as these arrangements do not result in quantitative copying sufficient to substitute for subscriptions or purchases of material.

Copyright experts find considerable ambiguity in these phrases and the activities they describe; some even find no significant difference between copying any and all articles individually as requested by users and making and retaining duplicate copies for quick retrieval when requests are submitted. Nevertheless, media specialists need to be aware of the distinction, however vague its specific application; and they are well advised to protect themselves against a strict interpretation of Section 108 by making copies only at the specific request of users or other libraries.

Computers and Copyright

Unless you have a license to do so, it is illegal to duplicate copies of software on disk, tape, or even in a computer's RAM (transient memory) so that two or more students can simultaneously utilize a program intended for a single user. That means that it is illegal to make multiple copies of a disk. It also is illegal to sequentially boot up a series of microcomputers with one disk, thereby enabling more than one student to access a program for which there is only one purchased disk, even though educators are not making duplicate copies. It is not uncommon for a teacher with sufficient computer knowledge to modify a piece of software so that several students can simultaneously access that program via a network of linked microcomputers. However, this networking arrangement violates the copyright law unless permission is obtained from the copyright owner to modify the work specifically for a microcomputer network.

To understand why unauthorized multiple booting up with one disk or networking from a single program designed for a single computer is illegal, some familiarity with the 1980 copyright amendments pertaining to computer software is necessary. Section 101 contains the definition of a computer program.

> A "computer program" is a set of statements or instructions to be used directly or indirectly in a computer in order to bring about a certain result.

How a computer program may be used is defined in Section 117.

Notwithstanding the provisions of section 106, it is not an infringement for the owner of a copy of a computer program to make or authorize the making of another copy or adaptation of that computer program provided:

(1) that such new copy or adaptation is created as an essential step in the utilization of the computer program in conjunction with a machine and that it is used in no other manner, or

(2) that such new copy or adaptation is for archival purposes only and that all archival copies are destroyed in the event that continued possession of the computer program should cease to be rightful.

Any exact copies prepared in accordance with the provisions of this section may be leased, sold, or otherwise transferred, along with the copy from which such copies were prepared, only as part of the lease, sale, or other transfer of all rights in the program. Adaptations so prepared may be transferred only with the authorization of the copyright owner.

A close reading of Section 117 discloses three different referents for the term *copy*. First, subsection (1) refers to the intangible copy in the computer's memory (RAM) made when the user inputs a piece of software into the computer. That copy, in most instances, disintegrates when the computer is turned off or when the user otherwise removes it from the central storage of the computer. Second, subsection (2) refers to the tangible, reproduced back-up copy made by the owner for archival purposes. And third, the opening qualifier of Section 117 refers to the owner's "copy of a computer program," which is the tangible piece of software, usually on disk, purchased by the user. To simplify our analysis, this user-owned copy will be referred to as the master copy and the tangibly reproduced copies will be referred to as duplicate copies.

Computer-law experts have given many differing — even contradictory — interpretations of Section 117. However, one point is indisputable: *absent permission from the copyright owner, it is illegal to make duplicate copies of a computer program for distribution to and use by anyone other than the owner of that master copy.* Conversely, the *only legal duplicated copy* of the master copy of a piece of software is the back-up copy made by the owner for archival purposes. This provision is intended to protect software users by ensuring that they will have a working copy of their program if the master copy is damaged or destroyed and must be sent to the manufacturer for repair or replacement.

While Section 117(2) permits the making of a single back-up copy, the law specifies that only the *owner* of a master copy can make or authorize the duplication of the back-up copy. That prohibits the duplication of one or more copies of a rented or borrowed program, since the user in those cases does not own the master copy. Therefore, *it is illegal to make a copy from a program acquired for preview purposes*. Finally, the back-up copy is legal only as an archival copy, not as a working copy to be used by someone else in another computer.

Section 117(1) defines the only other legally duplicated copy of an owner's master copy: that copy reproduced by inputting the program into the computer in order to utilize the program. Laypersons unfamiliar with copyright and computer terminology should know that 1) the inputting of a piece of software is considered to be making a copy, and 2) our legislators felt the need to include and protect such an obvious use. The rationale for this seemingly unnecessary provision is at least partially explained by the definition of the word *copy* contained in the copyright law; *copies* are defined as "material objects . . . in which a work is fixed"; and "[a] work is 'fixed' . . . when its embodiment in a copy . . . is sufficiently permanent or stable to permit it to be perceived, reproduced, or otherwise communicated for a period of more than transitory duration."

Given these definitions, the intangible computer program stored in the computer's memory in machine-readable form constitutes a reproduction from the tangible form of the program existing on a disk or tape. In order for the computer to perform its extended functions, a computer program must be transferred from its tangible form to the computer's memory for processing. Because a program in the memory of some computers can be accessed *and copied* by a user at a connecting terminal, and because it may be repeatedly reproduced or accessed, that intangible copy of a computer program existing in the machine's memory is considered a copy of a computer program. However difficult for laypeople to understand, this interpretation of what constitutes a copy has been accepted by nearly all legal and technical experts in the field of computer law.

Copyright and Software Use

Section 117 of the Copyright Act clearly prohibits the unauthorized duplication of a computer program for use by anyone other than the owner of a master copy. But Section 117 does not address the complexities of computer use in education. Fortunately, educators are not dependent solely on Section 117 for delineating the legal use of software in their schools. There are at least five other sources or tests for assessing the legality of the software uses mentioned above.

1. *The Market Effect Test.* Perhaps the first test — first both in order and in significance — for evaluating the legality of a questionable use of instructional software is the market effect test. Since an important function of the copyright law is to protect the financial interests of creative people, educators first should ask if their use of software results in economic harm to the copyright owner. To make or distribute duplicate copies from a master copy of a computer program not only violates Section 117 but fails the market effect test. It deprives the copyright owner of profits that otherwise would be earned from the sale of an equivalent number of copies of that program.

Applying the market effect test in other situations, we begin to see why some of the other educational uses of instructional software may be illegal. For example, a teacher who sequentially boots up a dozen microcomputers with one master copy of an instructional program is making it simultaneously accessible to 12 students, thereby depriving the copyright owner of profits from the sale of 11 additional copies of the program. Such use, unless authorized by the copyright owner or by accompanying license, fails the market effect test.

Likewise, a computer program designed for use in a single microcomputer but modified for a network of microcomputers deprives the copyright owner of profits from the sale of the number of copies equivalent to the number of stations being used simultaneously in the network. Therefore, simultaneous accessing by more than one person of a single-user program in a network also fails the market effect test. Educators should heed the Golden Rule for Computer Users, attributed to Joseph McDonald, which states: "Take not from others to such an extent and in such a manner that you would be resentful if they so took from you."

2. *The Intended Use Test*. The intended use test raises the question of the design of the program and the intention of its designer. This intended use test is especially helpful in resolving questions about the legality of networking computers. Specifically, if the program is *designed* and therefore intended to serve a network, such a use does not violate the copyright law. However, if the program is designed to be used by a single user at a single microcomputer and it is modified to serve multiple users in a network, it is not being used as intended, thereby failing the intended use test. The latter example has already been shown to fail the market effect test, making its legality doubly suspect.

3. *The Simultaneous/Sequential Users Test*. A third test suggested by some legal experts, most notably Daniel Brooks, distinguishes between simultaneous and sequential users. Though undoubtedly derived from the market effect and intended use tests, the distinction between simultaneous and sequential users further sharpens the legal analysis of such practices as networking and sequentially booting up a series of microcomputers with one disk. Essentially, under this test the use of a master copy by several persons is legal as long as they are accessing the program one at a time and not simultaneously. The rationale for this construction of the copyright law is based on the right of the *owner* of the master copy to do with that program what he or she wishes, as long as no duplicate copies are made (beyond the permissible back-up copy). That means that the owner of a WordStar program can loan the copy to any number of individuals, but only to one at a time.

Applying this principle to the school setting, a teacher with one master copy of a piece of instructional software might legally allow 12 students to use that master copy *one at a time* without fear of violating the copyright law, though allowing a dozen students to access that master copy simultaneously through a network or sequentially booting up a dozen microcomputers would constitute a copyright infringement.

However, close analysis of the reasoning behind the simultaneous/sequential users test raises the question of the *actual* difference between the two forms of allowing multiple users. It is true that the owner of a master copy may legally loan that copy to one or more individuals for their temporary use. And on an individual basis, such a practice would have only an inconsequential impact on the copyright owner. But in a classroom or computer lab in a school, the distinction between sequential and simultaneous multiple users begins to blur in terms of actual impact. The effect of a teacher providing a dozen students with simultaneous access to a modified computer program is not very different from the effect of a teacher allowing a dozen students to access a copy of that program one at a time. In *Columbia Pictures Industries, Inc.* v. *Redd Horne, Inc.* (1984) the Third Circuit Court of Appeals ruled this kind of distinction immaterial in a commercial setting, resulting in a violation of copyright law. The court found in this case that serial showings of videocassettes violated the copyright owner's exclusive right to perform the work publicly, which included members of the public receiving it "in the same place. . .at different times." In short, the distinction between sequential and simultaneous users is interesting and perhaps helpful, but it is not likely to produce the most decisive evidence if and when a software copyright case involving multiple users comes before the courts.

4. *Fair Use Test*. Educators will find it frustrating to apply the four factors governing fair use to computer software. In fact, there is little to encourage educators about applying fair use doctrine to justify duplication of instructional software in the schools.

The first factor, pertaining to the character and purpose of the use, might appear to be applicable from the perspective of educators, since they can usually meet the test of using copies of instructional software for educational, nonprofit purposes rather than for direct commercial benefit. However, as mentioned earlier, even the absence of profit does not, in itself, protect the person making duplicate copies.

The second fair use factor, the nature of the copyrighted work, is not applicable to instructional software because it is *designed for class-*

room use and is *easily accessible* for that use. Therefore, the copying of instructional software is clearly illegal.

The third fair use factor, the amount or portion of the original work that can be legally copied, is also not applicable, because it is nearly impossible to copy only part of a program from a floppy disk or any other medium containing a computer program. And even if it were possible to copy only part of a program, the partial copies would not be functional. In short, the only likely copying of a master disk involves copying the entire program. While copying entire works may conceivably constitute a fair use, it is not likely unless the copyrighted material is not otherwise reasonably accessible to the user.

Finally, the fourth factor pertaining to the effect of the use on the potential market is clearly not applicable to instructional software, because every copy made reduces the potential market and sales.

5. *Licensing Agreements.* The one remaining source for determining the legality of specific software use is the licenses that frequently accompany computer programs or sets of programs. These licenses may be found in manuals or other materials accompanying the disks, and they usually become effective when the packaging is unsealed. However, the legality of shrink-wrap licensing is currently being challenged in court.

Typical of the kind of license defining the legal use of software is this one from Spinnaker:

> The distribution and sale of this product are intended for the use of the original purchaser only and for use only on the computer system specified. Lawful users of this program are hereby licensed only to read the program from its medium into the memory of a computer for the purpose of executing this program. Copying, duplicating, selling or otherwise distributing this product is hereby expressly forbidden.

Although this license regulates the use of a single program by its owner, increasing numbers of instructional software producers are making a variety of licensing agreements to meet the needs of individual school districts. These agreements provide such financially beneficial options as 1) discounts for purchase of multiple copies, 2) permission to duplicate the number of copies required to meet student needs, and

3) designing software or granting permission to modify software for use in a computer network. Whatever the license provisions, users should understand that any licensing restrictions more stringent than the copyright law itself take precedence over that law.

Other Questioned Uses

Some educators have asked about the legality of making duplicate copies of a program for the purpose of introducing the software at a workshop or conference, after which the copies are erased. Rather than harming the copyright owner, they argue, they are actually enhancing the potential market by "seeding" the program to individuals who may purchase one or more copies of the software for use in their own school. This reasoning is not without merit; and it is possible that the software producer owning the copyright might concur with the reasoning, reducing the likelihood of prosecution for copyright infringement. Nevertheless, such copying is illegal; nothing in the copyright law provides for short-term duplication of a work in order to enlarge the potential market for that product. Once again, however, educators should remember that what the law prohibits can become legal if permission is obtained from the copyright holder.

School Libraries and Computer Software

Can professional staff in the libraries or media centers of education institutions loan copies of computer programs to students and faculty just as they loan books and other materials? Can they make additional duplicate copies of instructional software beyond the allowable back-up copy? If the working copy of a computer program is destroyed by a borrower, can the library make another working copy from its back-up copy? Can a school library stock its inventory with software that was illegally duplicated and then donated by a student or faculty member?

Section 117 of the Copyrights Act does not directly address library utilization of computer software, and there have been no judicial rulings pertaining to this question. Therefore, any answers must be tentative and based on a close reading of the statute for applications that can be implied from those developed for other copyrighted materials.

There is little reason to believe that libraries are prohibited from obtaining and loaning computer software. Nothing in Section 117 nor in any copyright decision prohibits the owner of a software program (in this case, the library) from loaning it to another individual as long as that individual does not make illegal copies. The library, like individual software owners, may make one back-up copy for archival purposes.

However, the right to duplicate copies ends with the back-up copy. Legal experts almost unanimously agree that for a library to *replace* a damaged copy with one that is duplicated from the back-up copy is illegal. But a library probably could make a *temporary* copy for use until a damaged or destroyed copy is replaced, provided that the temporary copy is erased on receipt of the replacement copy. No court or legislative body has addressed this question; but given the allowance for emergency copying of sheet music, it is reasonable to believe that if a library could document that it sent a purchase order or the damaged copy to the publisher for replacement, the temporary use of an otherwise illegally duplicated copy might be found a fair use.

Is it legal for a library to accept and then to loan illegally duplicated copies of computer software donated by students, parents, or faculty? Section 117 of the copyright law specifies that legally made copies of a program (back-up copies) may be transferred *along with the original copies* (master copies). Although not explicitly stated, one could assume that illegally made duplicate copies may not be transferred, which in essence is giving away stolen property. Therefore, the only donated copies of computer software a library may own would be the master copy and one back-up copy of each program.

Copyright Law and Audiovisual Materials

Copyright owners have the exclusive right to display and perform their works, including the projection of a film or videotape. However, educators may show films or videotapes without explicit permission from the copyright owner if those showings are for purely educational purposes, directly related to instruction, and shown only to students in a nonprofit education institution.

In order to know which uses of audiovisual materials are permitted and prohibited by the Copyrights Act, educators need to understand two key terms: *display* and *perform*. Section 101, which defines all major terms used in the Copyrights Act, contains these definitions:

> To "display" a work means. . .in the case of a motion picture or other audiovisual work, to show individual images nonsequentially.

> To "perform" a work means. . .in the case of a motion picture or other audiovisual work, to show its images in any sequence or to make the sounds accompanying it audible.

In layperson's terms, one "displays" pictures or individual frames from a film or videotape while one "performs" an audiovisual work by running all or part of it through the projector or recorder.

Permissible Uses

Since copyright proprietors are given the exclusive rights to display and perform their own works, educators would have trouble using any audiovisual materials legally were it not for Section 110. This provision contains an important exemption for educators by allowing:

> (1) performance or display of a work by instructors or pupils in the course of face-to-face teaching activities of a nonprofit educational institution, in a classroom or similar place devoted to instruction, unless, in the case of a motion picture or other audiovisual work, the performance, or the display of individual images is given by means of a copy that was not lawfully made...and that the person responsible for the performance knew or had reason to believe was not lawfully made.

Several ambiguities in this provision are clarified in the House report which contains definitions and descriptions of several terms. Section 110(4) also contains limitations that help clarify what is not permissible in terms of showing audiovisual materials on school property for other than direct instructional activities. Taken together, the House report and Section 110(1) and 110(4) are understood to permit displaying or performing audiovisual works *in nonprofit education institutions* under the following conditions:

1. They must be shown as part of the instructional program.
2. They must be shown by students, instructors, or guest lecturers.
3. They must be shown either in a classroom or other school location devoted to instruction such as a studio, workshop, library, gymnasium, or auditorium if it is used for instruction.
4. They must be shown either in a face-to-face setting or where students and teacher(s) are in the same building or general area.
5. They must be shown only to students and educators.
6. They must be shown using a legitimate (that is, not illegally reproduced) copy with the copyright notice included.

Prohibited Uses

Displays and performances of audiovisual works are prohibited in nonprofit education institutions when:

1. They are used for entertainment, recreation, or even for their cultural or intellectual value but are unrelated to teaching activity.

2. They are transmitted by radio or television (either closed or open circuit) from an outside location.
3. They are shown in an auditorium or stadium before an audience not confined to students, such as a sporting event, graduation ceremony, or community lecture or arts series.
4. They involve an illegally acquired or duplicated copy of the work.

Videotapes: The "For Home Use Only" Warning

As if educators' uneasiness with copyright restrictions were not sufficient, those who use videotapes may face the additional intimidation of a label that reads:

WARNING
"FOR HOME USE ONLY" MEANS JUST THAT!

Or the label may contain this warning:

Licensed only for non-commercial private exhibition in homes. Any public performance, other use, or copying is strictly prohibited.

Or a school may have received a notice from the Motion Picture Association of America (MPAA) warning that

[P]erformances in "semipublic" places such as clubs, lodges, factories, summer camps, and *schools* are "public performances" subject to copyright control. [emphasis added]

Are these warnings legitimate, misleading, or downright false? Are they binding? Do they apply to classroom use and to library use?

Most copyright experts find these warning labels neither binding nor an accurate representation of the rights of educators. Their position is based on Section 110(1), which grants educators the right to display or perform works in face-to-face learning situations, a right that cannot be taken away by an intimidating label.

Some educators may question whether the cassette labels, especially those beginning "Licensed only. . .," constitute a license, in which case the restriction supercedes Section 110(1). Metro-Goldwyn-Mayer/United Artists and other firms offer detailed purchase contracts or licenses that suggest the labels are merely advisory. And though no case has yet addressed this question, several cases have found *similar* labels to be inconsistent with the rights accompanying outright sale.

Educators should understand that the "For Home Use Only" warning on the label of many videotapes is unlikely to preclude using such tapes in their classrooms. The inclusion of schools in the MPAA's list of semipublic places subject to copyright restrictions applicable to "public performances" *does not preclude use in classroom instruction*; rather it applies to a showing held on school property, perhaps on an evening or weekend and open to the public, for entertainment or for cultural purposes. A public performance on school property is not the same as instructional activities limited to students. The effect of these warnings is to confuse public performance with classroom instruction, leading to the misperception that the restriction applies to the classroom when, in fact, it may apply only to school showings open to the public or to showings for entertainment or non-instructional activities for students.

School Libraries and Videotapes

It is not yet clear whether libraries can legally allow users to view videotapes on equipment within the library itself. Copyright owners have the exclusive right to perform their works publicly, and the showing of a videotape constitutes a performance. However, there is ambiguity in the interpretation of the word *publicly*.

As defined in Section 101, to perform or display a work publicly involves "a place open to the public" or "any place where a substantial number of persons outside of a normal circle of a family and its social acquaintances is gathered." This definition was intended to make explicit the right of users to perform, or view, audiovisual works in their homes. However, the Third Circuit Court of Appeals in *Redd Horne* recently upheld a lower court ruling that the seriatum viewings of individuals or small groups (no more than four viewers) in an establishment open to the public constituted an infringement "because the potential exists for a substantial portion of the public to attend such performances over a period of time." However, because this case involved a commercial establishment, its applicability to libraries is neither direct nor clear.

School libraries can allow videotapes to be viewed by teachers or students provided that such viewing is for instructional purposes. Presumably this applies to viewings by individual or small groups of students as part of a class assignment or project. But random viewings in the library or media center that are not related directly to instruction may be questionable, unless of course the media specialist or other school personnel obtains permission through license or contract to so use its videotapes. Until there is futher clarification, school libraries may be best advised to allow the viewing of videotapes in library carrels or rooms only for directly instructional purposes rather than for random viewing or entertainment by students or teachers.

The *loaning* of videotapes by libraries to users for use in their own homes poses no legal problems. Libraries have the right to sell, *loan*, or otherwise dispose of their copies.

The *reproduction* of videotapes by libraries is limited by restrictions in Section 108. Libraries may reproduce and distribute videotapes only to replace a work that is lost, stolen, or damaged and that cannot otherwise be replaced at a fair price.

School Libraries and Other Audiovisual Materials

The *performance* of films and filmstrips and the display of individual images are not governed by the restrictions applicable to videotapes because of practices established well before the 1976 copyright revision. For years film companies have sold nontheatrical — and especially educational — films to education institutions under contractual arrangements that permit showing their films as long as no fees are charged to viewers. Theatrical films were not sold but distributed through licensing agreements. Given the decades of experience with these approaches to distributing motion pictures to schools, film companies have chosen to continue this practice with films and filmstrips. However, when the 1976 Copyrights Act provided new protections for copyright proprietors' rights to perform their works, the industry did find it advantageous to enforce those rights through the videotape restrictions described above.

The *reproduction* of audiovisual materials by libraries is, like the reproduction of printed materials, governed by Section 108. This provision of the copyright law treats audiovisual and visual artistic works somewhat differently from written materials, placing greater limitations on the visual and audiovisual works. Specifically, a library may reproduce and distribute a musical work; a pictorial, graphic, or sculptural work; or a motion picture or other audiovisual work (except audiovisual news programs) *only* to replace a work that is lost, stolen, damaged, or deteriorating and that cannot otherwise be replaced at a fair price. If any of these works is unpublished, it may also be reproduced in facsimile form (that is, in the same medium as the owned copy) for purposes of preservation, security, or deposit for research in another library.

Libraries also may provide users with reproductions of pictorial or graphic works published as illustrations in copyrighted works that are legally reproduced or distributed.

While Section 108 specifically limits to *one copy* the number of copies that may be duplicated for replacement, preservation, or deposit in another library, there is one exception to this limitation: audiovisual news programs, which may be reproduced and distributed in limited quantities rather than only one copy. However, the reproduction and distribution of these copies are subject to the same qualifications as the single copy duplication. There must be no intent to obtain financial advantage; the library must be open to the public or, if it is a specialized research library or archives, it must at least be open to researchers; and notice of copyright must be included in the copies.

Videotape Recorders: Off-Air Taping

Increasing numbers of educators are supplementing their classroom instruction with videotaped copies of programs produced by both commercial and public television broadcasting corporations. While videotaping television programs off the air for later showing in classrooms can supplement and enrich the curriculum at all levels of schooling, educators must strictly follow certain guidelines. There are two sets of guidelines that educators should understand, one set for commercial broadcasts and a slightly different set for programs broadcast by four major public television services.

Guidelines for Taping Commercial Broadcasts

The guidelines for videotaping commercial broadcasts are contained in the "Guidelines for Off-the-Air Recording of Broadcast Programming for Educational Purposes." Ratified in 1981 by the House Subcommittee on the Courts, Civil Liberties, and the Administration of Justice, these guidelines are considered a retroactive part of the legislative history of the 1976 Copyrights Act. Although they do not have the force of law, they can be expected to serve as primary criteria when courts assess fair use in any future cases involving off-air videotaping for educational purposes.

Although there are a number of restrictions placed on the use of videotaped television programs, the two most critical limitations are:

1. Videotaped recordings may be kept for no more than *45 calendar days* after the recording date, at which time the tapes must be erased.
2. Videotaped recordings may be shown to students only within the *first 10 school days* of the 45-day retention period.

Additional restrictions that must be followed include:

3. Off-air recordings must be made only *at the request* of an individual teacher for *instructional* purposes, not by school staff in anticipation of later requests by teachers.
4. The recordings are to be shown to students no more than two times during the 10-day period, and the second time only for necessary instructional reinforcement.
5. The taped recordings may be viewed after the 10-day period only by teachers for evaluation purposes, that is, to determine whether to include the broadcast program in the curriculum in the future.
6. If several teachers request videotaping of the same program, duplicate copies are permitted to supply their request; all copies are subject to the same restrictions as the original recording.
7. The off-air recordings may not be physically or electronically altered or combined with others to form anthologies, but they need not necessarily be used or shown in their entirety.
8. All copies of off-air recordings must include the copyright notice on the broadcast program as recorded.
9. These guidelines apply only to nonprofit education institutions, which are further "expected to establish appropriate control procedures to maintain the integrity of these guidelines."

These guidelines apply to all commercial television broadcasts and to some public broadcasts. Educators should also remember that these guidelines are *operative only in the absence of licensing agreements*, which themselves may be either more or less restrictive than the guidelines. To obtain a license to use off-air videotaped programs for more than 45 days, contact the Television Licensing Center (TLC), 5447 N. Ravenswood Ave., Chicago, IL 60640. Licensing agreements with TLC are less costly than buying tapes from the broadcast corporations.

Educators employed in intermediate-level state education agencies must also be aware of a series of recent court decisions involving one such agency in the state of New York. The case is familiarly known by the name of the defendant agency, Board of Cooperative Educational Services (BOCES). After years of judicial entanglement, the court ruled in 1982 and 1983 that the agency violated copyright law by its large-scale and systematic off-air videotaping of broadcast programs, duplication and retention of those copies, and distribution of copies to all schools in its service region that requested copies. Although it is a nonprofit agency and provided schools with only educational videotaped films, the court held that their activity did not constitute a fair use. Key factors in the court's consideration were not only the scope of copying and distribution (duplication of 10,000 videotapes in two years) but also the potential harm to the copyright owners, who made their films available to schools for short-term rental or lease.

In short, education agencies and schools may engage in short-term, intermittent off-air videotaping following the federal guidlines; but they may not engage in long-term, systematic, large-scale taping. From the guidelines it also is obvious that, absent permission, schools may not build library collections of videotapes of television programs.

Guidelines for Taping Public Broadcasting Service Programs

Before the enactment of the 1976 Copyrights Act, four public broadcasting services drew up a joint policy statement that allows schools specific videotaping privileges for their productions. These four services are Public Broadcasting Service, Public Television Library, Great Plains National Instructional Television Library, and Agency for Instructional Television. For programs distributed by these four entities, educators may record their broadcasts on the following conditions:

1. The recordings may be made only by students, faculty, or staff members in accredited, nonprofit education institutions.
2. The recordings may be used only for instruction or educationally related activities in a classroom, laboratory, or auditorium.

3. The recordings may be used only in the school for which they were made; they may not be made available outside that school.

4. The recordings may be used "only during the seven-day period of local ETV [Educational Television] and other educational broadcast licensed by the distribution agency, and will be erased or destroyed immediately at the end of that seven-day period except to the extent specifically authorized in writing in advance."

These public broadcasting guidelines are similar to the off-air guidelines for commercial broadcasts in that the recordings must be requested by teachers and shown only to students and faculty for instructional purposes. They differ from the commercial broadcasting off-air guidelines by not restricting the showings to students in the class taught by the requesting teacher. A teacher could request the taping of a public broadcast program and show the recording to the entire school, provided that the program served instructional rather than entertainment purposes. Also, these recordings may be kept for only seven days, although the number of showings is not limited.

Television Broadcasts Taped by Teachers

Educators who videotape a televised program in their homes and show the tapes to their classes should probably follow the guidelines applicable to off-air taping by schools until a specific court ruling or legislation directly addresses this particular activity. There have not yet been any cases raising this problem for judicial consideration, but it is possible to analyze the problem on the basis of factors already established. First, the 1984 Supreme Court *Sony* decision affirmed the right of individuals to use videocassette recordings in their homes; this right was upheld primarily on the basis of "private, noncommercial time-shifting in the home." But the majority did not address the use of privately taped programs for public performances or for educational purposes, and four justices did dissent from the majority opinion. However, their argument in the dissent could be interpreted to provide even more support for use of privately taped programs in the schools. Justice Blackmun, writing the dissent, considered off-air taping for the benefit and convenience of a single individual to be far less worthy of protection or a finding of fair use than the off-air taping by an individual for *productive* uses. This emphasis on using a copyrighted work for the public benefit is frequently a major consideration of the courts in determining fair use.

Two other closely related questions might prove critical in resolving the problem of videotapes made by teachers and used in classrooms. Taken from the guidelines adopted as acceptable fair use standards, these are questions we might expect a court to consider: "Did the teacher show this videotape once or twice for instructional purposes and then erase that tape? Or did the teacher retain the videotape for several months or years, showing it to classes each semester over a period of time?" While it cannot be said that even the more conservative of these practices is legal, it seems reasonable to assume that teachers taping at home and otherwise following the guidelines required for schools are more likely to be granted a finding of fair use than teachers who tape at home and otherwise violate the guidelines for off-air taping. Reasonable assumptions, however, are just that and must not be confused with explicit legal declarations.

The primary restriction to be kept in mind is that such off-air videotapes should not be retained and shown repeatedly over one or more semesters. A more liberal construction of fair use in this situation may be rendered in the future; but until that time, educators should follow the more strict construction of fair use in showing home-taped broadcasts in their classrooms.

Live and Transmitted Performances

Although the projection of a moving picture is considered a performance under the copyright law, the word *perform* also covers more common activities. To perform a work, according to Section 101, is to "recite, render, play, dance, or act it, either directly or by means of any device or process."

Live Performances

The 1976 revisions of the copyright law considerably expanded the rights of educators to perform copyrighted materials without special permission. Specifically, Section 110(4) permits the performance of a *nondramatic literary or musical work* when the following conditions are met:

1. The performance is live, rather than transmitted from another location.
2. The purpose of the performance is not the direct or indirect commercial advantage to the sponsor of the performance.
3. There is no payment to performers, promoters, or organizers of the performance (not applicable to a salaried music teacher leading a student production or other comparable instance).
4. There is no admission charge or, if admission is charged, all proceeds, after deducting reasonable costs, are used exclusively for educational, religious, or charitable purposes.

These qualifications apply strictly to the privileged performance of nondramatic literary and musical works. Audiovisual works and drama, by exclusion from this provision, may not be performed without permission from the copyright owner.

Transmitted Performances

A transmitted performance is one for which the "images or sounds are received beyond the place from which they are sent." In essence, it is a performance transmitted by radio or television. Section 110(2) limits the transmission of nondramatic literary or musical copyrighted works much the same as it does the live performance of such works. Again, this privilege, however limited, does not extend to dramatic or audiovisual works. In order for transmitted performances of these works to be legal, they must:

1. be a part of the "systematic instructional activities" (that is, related to the curriculum) of a nonprofit education institution that is transmitting them for noncommercial purposes;
2. be received in classrooms or other instruction-related places, or be received by persons unable to attend classes at an education institution site because of disabilities or other special circumstances (interpreted to include those who are responsible for caring for pre-school-age children);
3. be transmitted through either a cable system, a noncommercial educational broadcast station, or a radio subcarrier authorization.

One further exemption is made for the radio transmission of *dramatic* literary works via a radio subcarrier authorization. This exemption permits one reading (not repeated readings) on the radio of a dramatic work at least 10 years old in programming directed to the blind.

Penalties for Infringement of Copyright

Educators, education institutions, and school districts may be sued if they infringe or violate the rights of a copyright owner. In a suit for copyright violations, the court initially may issue an injunction to prohibit further reproduction or distribution of the work in question. The court also may impound all allegedly illegal copies of the copyrighted work; and if charges of infringement are later substantiated, the court may order the destruction or disposal of those illegal copies.

At any time before the court's final judgment, the copyright owner may elect to recover statutory damages; and if the defendent is found liable, the court awards at its discretion an amount ranging from $250 to $10,000. The amount of statutory damages awarded to the copyright owner varies with the facts of the case:

1. If the court finds that the infringer committed the infringing acts willfully, it may award damages up to $50,000.
2. If the court finds that the "infringer was not aware and had no reason to believe that his or her acts constituted an infringement of copyright," it may reduce the award of damages to not less than $100.
3. If the infringer is an employee of an education institution, library, or archives and had reason to believe that the reproduc-

tion of copies constituted a fair use, the court will automatically award statutory damages. Although the copyright law provision does not specify the range of damages to be awarded, it is reasonable to expect that such action would be considered comparable to unknowing infringement, with statutory damages of no less than $100.

Finally, although there is little likelihood of purely educational uses of copyrighted materials resulting in criminal charges of copyright violation, educators still should be aware that such charges can be brought. If they are found guilty of willfully infringing a copyright for private or commercial financial gain, they could be fined up to $10,000 or imprisoned for up to one year or both. Also unlikely, but a possibility of which educators should be aware, is the option of the copyright owner to sue for actual rather than statutory damages. In this case, he or she will attempt to recover damages actually suffered and any profits accruing to the infringer. Unless the educator has been engaged in some form of private enterprise, his or her profits will be nonexistent. And except for grossly extensive reproduction of expensive computer software or audiovisual materials, the actual damages suffered by a copyright owner from an educator's infringement will be minimal. These last two instances render highly unlikely the chances of educators being liable for actual rather than statutory damages.

Conclusion

Educators have a special need to familiarize themselves with the copyright law, especially since recent technological developments have rendered copyrighted material so susceptible to quick, easy, and cheap duplication. Although the intricacies of this law may seem intimidating, the essentials presented in this fastback provide the basis for compliance with copyright restrictions.

Quick reference to this fastback can answer many questions about the use or duplication of copyrighted materials in education. But when a question arises, educators should always ask the question most likely to be considered by the courts: Will duplication of the material substitute for the use or purchase of the original in such a way as to cause economic injury to the copyright holder? If so, they seriously jeopardize their chances for a finding of fair use. The other question to be addressed is whether the copyrighted material in question is in fact protected by the copyright law or by a license. If a license exists, the specific licensing provisions determine the legal and illegal uses of the work.

Up to now, lack of specific information has been a factor in the copyright violations involving educators. But as this information becomes more readily available, the only explanation for violations will be presumed to be deliberate noncompliance. Even when the motive for a violation is altruistic (for example, providing materials for students while saving taxpayer dollars), such noncompliance not only endangers the educational enterprise but undermines the image commonly referred to in education law as "teacher as exemplar."

Rather than expecting teachers to be solely responsible for compliance with copyright law, administrators and school boards also should accept some responsibility. They should adopt precise policies for the legal use of technology in their schools, colleges, and universities. They also can arrange for inservice workshops or seminars on copyright issues. An invaluable resource in most districts or institutions is the media specialist who belongs to a professional association that makes accurate and up-to-date information about copyright a high priority.

Restrictive as the copyright law may seem, the fair use provision offers substantial exemptions that enable educators to use needed materials. The four fair use factors (character and purpose of the use, nature of the copyrighted work, extent and significance of copied portion, and market effect) are helpful, but they are vague and sometimes result in unpredictable applications. On the other hand, the various guidelines adopted for photocopying and off-air videotaping provide highly specific criteria for determining fair use, even though these guidelines do not have the force of law. Copyright law and established guidelines may place constraints on educators, but laws and guidelines are not immutable. Education groups might initiate efforts to work with Congress to modify these laws and guidelines. However, until such modifications are adopted, educators must recognize and observe the legal requirements and ethical implications of copyright law.

References

Columbia Pictures Industries, Inc. v. Redd Horne, Inc., 749 F.2d 154 (1984).

Copyright and Educational Media: A Guide to Fair Use and Permissions Procedures. Washington, D.C.: Association for Educational Communications and Technology, 1977.

Copyrights Act. 17 U.S.C. 101 to 810 (1976 & Cum. Supp. 1984).

Encyclopaedia Britannica Educational Corporation v. Crooks [BOCES], 542 F.Supp. 1156 (W.D.N.Y. 1982), 558 F.Supp. 1247 (W.D.N.Y. 1983).

Helm, Virginia M. *Software Quality and Copyright: Issues in Computer-Assisted Instruction*. Washington, D.C.: Association for Educational Communications and Technology, 1984.

Johnston, Donald F. *The Copyright Handbook*, 2nd ed. New York: R.R. Bowker Company, 1982. (See Chapter 14, "Copyrights and Teaching Activities")

Miller, Jerome K. *Using Copyrighted Videocassettes in Classrooms and Libraries*. Friday Harbor, Wash.: Copyright Information Services, 1984.

Miller, Jerome K. *The Copyright Directory*. Friday Harbor, Wash.: Copyright Information Services, 1984.

The Official Fair-Use Guidelines: Complete Texts of Four Official Documents Arranged for Use by Educators. Friday Harbor, Wash.: Copyright Information Services, 1985.

Sinofsky, Esther R. *Off-Air Videotaping in Education: Copyright Issues, Decisions, Implications*. New York: R.R. Bowker Company, 1984.

Sony Corporation of America, et al. v. Universal City Studios, Inc., 104 S.Ct. 774 (1984).

Williams & Wilkins Co. v. United States, 420 U.S. 376 (1975).